DOG ON A LOG™
Chapter Books
Step 9

This is a work of fiction. Names, characters, places, and incidents are either products of the author's imagination or are used fictitiously. Any resemblance to actual persons, living or dead, businesses, companies, events, or locales is entirely coincidental.

DOG ON A LOG Books
Tucson, Arizona

Copyright ©2020 By Pamela Brookes
All Rights Reserved.
For information, contact the publisher at
read@dogonalogbooks.com

Photo credits on page 371

Public Domain images from
www.clker.com

ISBN: 978-1949471816

Library of Congress Control Number:
2020900478

www.dogonalogbooks.com

FOUR CHAPTER BOOKS
9

By Pamela Brookes

Download DOG ON A LOG printable gameboards, games, flashcards, and other activities at:
www.dogonalogbooks.com/printables.

Parents and Teachers:
Receive email notifications of new books and printables. Sign up at:
www.dogonalogbooks.com/subscribe

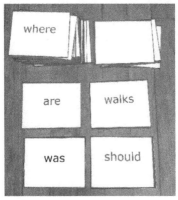

Table of Contents

DOG ON A LOG
Parent and Teacher Guides

General Information on Dyslexia and Struggling Readers

The Author's Routine for Teaching Reading

Book 1. *Teaching a Struggling Reader: One Mom's Experience with Dyslexia*

Book 2. *How to Use Decodable Books to Teach Reading*

Available for free from many online booksellers or read at:
www.dogonalogbooks.com/free

TRIP TO CACTUS GULCH 1: THE STEP-UP TEAM

Read to Me Dogs

Jan told her mom, "I want to help kids get **Read to Me Dogs**."

When she said that, she did not know what would happen.

She did not know that she and her friends would hike 1,000 steps.

She did not know they would go into a mineshaft.

Most of all, she did not know that it would be so epic.

Cash for Dogs

The Public Hall for Tomes of Tales has a note on its wall. The note has a snapshot of Tup and says, "Read to Me."

Tup is a **Read to Me Dog**. Each week, Jan and Gret's mom takes Tup to **The Public Hall for Tomes of Tales**. Lots of kids like to read to Tup.

Some kids read long tales about boats that go to islands.

Some kids read tales that are not long. They could be about a cat or a dog or a set of kids with a box.

Some kids do not read yet. They tell Tup about the snapshots in the volumes they like best.

Tup wags his tail when the kids read to him. He likes his job as a **Read to Me Dog**. He likes it when kids pet him and say, "Thank you, Tup. See you next week."

Jan and Gret go with their mom and Tup. Each week they sit at a desk where they can see their mom. They do not sit so close to Tup. They want the kids to feel free to read to Tup.

From time to time, a kid will walk past Jan and Gret and say, "I wish I could have a dog. I would like a dog to read to at home."

Jan and Gret feel sad when kids say stuff like that. They wish that all kids could have a **Read to Me Dog** like Tup.

* * *

Tup has just had a grand day as a **Read to Me Dog**. Ten kids came to read to him.

Tup has just had a grand day as a
Read to Me Dog.

It is time for Tup and his people to go home.

Tup, Jan, and Gret's home is ten miles from **The Public Hall for Tomes of Tales**. Their home is in the wildlands where snakes, bobcats, and skunks have their homes as well.

Tup jumps onto the back seat of the van. Jan, Gret, and Mom click their seat belts.

"Each kid should have a dog they can read to," Gret tells her Mom. "It makes me sad that not all kids can have a dog."

"Not all people want dogs. It takes a lot of time and cash to have a dog," Mom says. She backs the van out of the lot and drives onto the street.

"Then they should have a plush dog they can read to," Gret says.

"It takes cash to get a plush dog. Not all moms and dads have that much cash. We have grand luck that we have cash for a fine home and a grand dog like Tup," Mom says.

"I want to help kids get **Read to Me Dogs**," Jan says. "Could we go to a shop and get some plush dogs for the kids that read to Tup?"

"Tup had ten kids read to him this day. Some days he does not see that set of kids. I think he has had about one hundred kids come read to him. If we get a plush dog for each kid that reads to him, it would be a lot of cash. Then we would not have cash left to get stuff for Tup to eat," Mom says.

"What if we get jobs?" Gret says.

"We are just kids. We cannot get jobs," Jan says.

"You cannot get jobs, but you could find ways to get cash," Mom says. "Let us think about that. I bet we could find a way to get cash for plush **Read to Me Dogs** to gift to kids that want them. You could do a 'Please Fund Us' run or some such thing."

The Plan

Liv cannot walk. She gets from here to there on a seat with wheels. She grasps the rims of her wheels and with a push she glides up the hall. She goes out the exit and down the ramp.

This is the day. Liv cannot wait. She and her friends will go to the small hamlet of Cactus Gulch.

When they get there, they will dine then sleep at **The Mules' Bed and Brunch Inn**.

When the sun comes up, it will be time for **The Step-Up Team** to hike the steps of Cactus Gulch. Liv, her mom, and her dad will be in one of the sag vans. They will have drinks and snacks for **The Step-Up Team**.

Jan and Gret came up with the plan for **The Step-Up Team**. Each kid that is on **The Team** will hike 1,000 steps in Cactus Gulch.

All the kids gave a call to their moms' and dads' friends. They said they would like to make cash to get plush **Read to Me Dogs** for kids that do not have dogs.

The kids all said they had an ask. Their ask is for a gift of cash for each step they hike. With the cash, **The Step-Up Team** can get plush **Read to Me Dogs** for kids that need them.

Most people have said they will give a dime for each ten steps the kids hike. If they hike 1,000 steps, they will get $10 from each friend that said they would fund the hike.

When Jan and Gret had told Liv about **The Step-Up Team**, she was sad. "I cannot walk. I cannot get cash for plush dogs," she had said.

"We have a plan for that. You cannot walk and Jeff and Chuck cannot see," Jan had said.

"The steps in Cactus Gulch have cracks and are steep. The steps are not safe for them. We must have sag vans to hand us water and snacks and tell us we cannot stop or sleep," Gret had said.

"We must have a team that tells us we must go to the next set of steps. We trust you, Jeff, and Chuck. We need you to be in the sag vans. With you there, we can trust we will get a drink and a snack," Jan had said.

"Plus, we did think of a way for you to make cash. There will be 31 people on **The Step-Up Team**. Ten kids and six sets of moms and dads will hike the steps. That is 22 people," Jan says.

"And three dogs. Tup, Bade, and Ms. Jolt," Gret had said.

"Yes, there will be dogs as well. All the people and dogs will drink a lot of water that you, Jeff, and Chuck must hand out. We will get cash for all the steps we hike, but you can get cash for all the drinks you hand out," Jan had said.

That had made Liv glad. She gave a call to all her mom's and dad's friends. When she did the math to add up all the gifts, she could see she would get a lot of cash for plush **Read to Me Dogs**.

Liv wheels back up the ramp into her home. "Is it time to go?" she asks her dad.

"Yes, it is. We will meet the rest of **The Step-Up Team** at the Truckstop on the way to Cactus Gulch. We will all get gas then be on our way," Liv's dad says.

Liv wheels out to the van. She cannot wait to meet with her friends.

The Drive

The Step-Up Team drives about one hundred miles to Cactus Gulch. The road twists here and there. It goes up one hill and down the next.

It is spring and the trees are green. The stick cactus have buds like flames on their tips.

Each cactus has buds that are white, pink, and gold. The tallest cactus reach up to the sun.

The kids split into vans so that there will be, at most, one dog in each van. Jan, Gret, Mave, Colt, their moms and dads, and Tup are all in one van.

The kids sing songs and tell jokes.

Some of the jokes make the moms and dads smile. Some of the jokes are odd and the moms and dads do not get them. Then the kids have to tell them what the joke means.

Mave and Colt's dad says, "I think we are so old we do not get some of your jokes."

When the vans reach the top of the last hill, all the vans pull into the rest stop.

They all get out to see the hamlet of Cactus Gulch.

There are old homes on the side of the hills.

The gulch runs next to the road. There is a fast stream that cascades down the gulch.

The shops and homes have coats of paint with tints so grand that **The Step-Up Team** can see the paint all the way up here.

Cactus Gulch was made next to a mine. The mine would smelt the rocks so they would run like water. Then it was made into water pipes and plugs for TVs and stoves.

Then the best rocks ran out. The rocks could not smelt into pipes and such. The mine had to shut down.

All the people that had jobs in the mine had to sell their homes and go find jobs a long way from here.

When the mine shut down, the homes in Cactus Gulch got made into shops and public halls.

The grandest homes got made into **The Mules' Bed and Brunch Inn** and the **Sleep and Rest Here Inn**.

The Step-Up Team plans to take one day for the Step-Hike and the next day for a trip into the mineshaft

"It does not seem unsafe," Fran says as she scans Cactus Gulch from the rest stop. "I think Jeff and Chuck could hike the steps with us."

"No. The steps are old and not made well. They lean and have cracks," Chuck's mom says.

"It is safe if you can see where you step and hold onto the hand rail. Jeff and Chuck could not see where to step. They could stub a toe or twist their legs and fall," Jeff's mom says.

"We need Chuck and Jeff to help with the sag vans," Jan says.

"My grandpop says there are lots of odd things in this hamlet," Brad says.

"Hamlet? Like Dennis and Robin Hamlet?" Liz asks.

"Yes, their name is the same," Liz's dad says.

"Well, our grandpop says there is so much odd stuff we will not see it all," Fran says.

"Then he told us that he would gift us cash for **Read to Me Dogs** if we kept a list of all the odd stuff we see as we hike up the steps," Brad says.

"I have pens and notepads so we can jot down all the odd stuff we see," Fran says.

"That is a grand plan," Mave says.

"Clop, clop, groan, groan."

A truck drives past the kids, moms, dads, and dogs. It pulls a stack of old crates on planks set on wheels.

Some of the crates have bits of black or green paint, some are plain tan.

Each stack of crates has five or six crates. They are tied down with red straps. On the back of the stack is a plank that says, "Home Sweet Home."

"That was odd," Dave says.

"Is that a small home made from crates?" Fran asks.

"I think it could be," Fran's dad says.

"Can we put that on the list of odd things or must we wait for when we hike the steps?" Mave asks.

"I did not think to ask Grandpop," Brad says.

"I think we should have two lists. One will be what we see when we hike the steps. One will be what we see the rest of the trip. We can ask Grandpop when we get home," Fran says.

"Let us get in our vans and go to **The Mules' Bed and Brunch Inn**. I want to take a bath and go out to dine," Jan's dad says.

Cactus Gulch

As they drive into Cactus Gulch, **The Step-Up Team** scans the hamlet. The shops and homes are old. They are made from brick. The panes of glass have waves and some have a tint of green. The shops are all on roads in a line. The homes are up on the hills.

They drive past the shops and go up a hill past the old homes. A man walks with two mules. Each mule is on a leash. The mules eat the grass next to the road.

"Jot down 'Mules on leash' on the odd thing list," Colt tells Mave.

Next to the road there are steel posts. Ropes are strung from one post to the next. The ropes help people see the deep gulch.

At the base of the gulch are plants, trees, and rocks. The water goes fast from rock to rock.

"That rope does not seem like it would keep a kid safe. I would think they could fall into the stream," Jan says. "I do not think that is for the list of odd things. Odd things are fun. I would not like to fall down there."

"The rope is not for the list, but do you see that home? It spans the gulch. When they walk there, they walk on top of the gulch," Gret says.

"I think that bit of the home that spans the gulch is the truck-shed where they put their trucks and vans," Jan says.

"Mom, is it odd that people would put their trucks and vans on top of a gulch?" Gret asks. She smiles. "It must be odd if I need to ask that."

As they get to **The Mules' Bed and Brunch Inn**, there are two big trees that seem to greet them. Each leaf sways in a bit of wind as if they are hands that wave, "Hi."

"Should we take time to rest and have baths? We could go dine at 6:00. I saw a sandwich shop as we drove in. We can walk there and..." Liz's mom says then stops. The man with the mules walks up to them.

"Hi. Welcome to **The Mules' Bed and Brunch Inn**. This is Jonquil and this is Doe," he says as he pats the mules.

"Well, I will be," Liz's mom says. "We have colts and oxen, but I must admit I have not got to stand next mules. They seem so big."

"Jonquil and Doe are sweet. You can all pet them," the man says.

The kids pet the mules. "Did you name the bed and brunch for the mules?" Fran asks.

"No. They had mules in the mine. We got the name from the mine mules," the man says.

"We will go into the mine in two days," Fran says.

"In two days? That will be a grand time to go into the mine. You have the best luck," the man says with a smile. "You will be so glad you get to go that day," the man says.

"What happens that day?" Liv's dad asks.

The man smiles. "I cannot say. All the hamlet has said we cannot say. If we said, lots of people would vie to go that day. You will be glad you get to go that day. I bet you would like to check in. I will tie up the mules then help you."

The   Step-Up   Team
checks in. They each take a
bath, then they all dine.

As they eat, they talk
about the mine trip. The
man that brings them stuff
to eat smiles when they
talk about the mine.

When they ask the man
what he knows about the
mine, he just smiles and
says, "You will be glad you
get to go into the mine that
day."

Get Set and GO!

Jan wakes to "Tweet, tweet," from a finch. It is in the tree just past the glass pane next to her bed. Tup lies on the bed next to her. He wags his tail when he sees she is up.

"I will let you out, but do not chase that finch," Jan tells Tup.

Tup runs to a tree. Bade and Ms. Jolt sniff the base of the tree. When they see Tup, they jump and run. The three dogs run from one side of the lot to the next.

Some of **The Step-Up Team** sit next to the pond or a tree, some are still inside. Mave, Colt, their mom, and dad sit next to a shrub that has pink buds.

"Hi," Colt says to Jan and waves to her. "Fran and her mom went to pick up stuff for us to eat. They will be back in just a bit. There will be toast, beans, grits, fried spuds, and lots of stuff."

"That will be grand," Jan says as she goes back inside to wake Gret.

The Step-Up Team makes a line of all they will eat on a picnic bench. They fill their plates and eat until they cannot eat the next bite. They all want to be strong for their 1,000-Step-Hike.

They finish their meal then clean up. They dress in clothes for their hike, get in the vans, and drive to Step Set One.

Jan's dad has the print out of the Step-Hike Map. He got it online. It will tell **The Team** which steps to hike. It will say which steps they must hike to get to 1,000 steps.

The vans stop at Step-Set One. The kids all gaze up at the steps.

The steps are steep with a rail on one side. The steps go up then zag to the left then go up, up, up.

Some of the steps are tall, some have cracks. The rail they will hold is made from old pipe. The rail's gray paint has chips that let them see white and black specks of old paint.

"That is a lot of steps," Quin says.

"The Step-Hike map says there are 83 steps," Jan's dad says.

"Just 83? It seems like there are a lot of steps, not just 83," Jan says.

"Mom, Dad, and I will be at the top. We will have snacks for you," Liv says.

"Yes, Liv. Let us drive up to the road to the top of the steps. I think the road is long and steep to get all the way up there," Liv's dad says.

Liv, Jeff, Chuck, and their moms and dads all drive to the step tops where they will greet **The Step-Up Team**.

"Can we jot down the zigzag steps as odd?" Gret asks. "They zig and zag from side to side. They do not just go up. Plus, their rails are like waves. They do not go in a flat line. They go up to a post then down to the next post."

"Yes, jot it down. If Grandpop does not think they are odd, he will not gift us cash," Brad says.

The kids had a vote. Lil will jot down all the odd things **The Team** sees. She gets out her notepad and pen. "I put it on the list of odd stuff," she tells her friends.

"OK. Are you all set? Is it time for the Step-Hike?" Jan's dad asks.

The Team all nod and yell, "Yes!"

"OK, then. Let us GET SET," Jan's dad says, then stops and scans **The Step-Up Team**. "AND GO!" Jan's dad yells.

567 Steps

Tup, Bade, and Ms. Jolt can feel their people are glad so the dogs all go, "Ruff, ruff."

Kids, moms, dads, and dogs go to the steps. They each grab the rail and get on the steps.

Dave and Colt vie to lead the way, then Bade pulls on his leash to get past Dave. Jan and Tup are with Quin and Fran. Gret, Liz, and Lil are at the back.

Ms. Jolt goes, "Ruff, ruff." She wants to keep up with Tup and Bade.

Jan is on one step, then the next. This step is tall and she must reach and grab the rail then pull to get on it.

The next step has a crack and it is not flat. Jan gets up on the next step and slips.

"Mom. Do you see this? The top of this step was made with bits of glass." Then she calls back to Lil, "Can you add this glass step to the list of odd stuff?"

"Yes, I can," Lil calls as she gets her notepad.

At the top of the steps, **The Team** stops for drinks of water. They do not need snacks. Liv hands each of the team a cup with their name on it. When they have had their drinks water, she takes the cup so they will have it at her next stop.

The Team walks up the street to the next set of steps.

"Do you see that wall?" Mave asks. "It is made from an old bed and...I cannot tell what that is. It has so much rust."

"That is a truck frame," Mave's dad says. "Do you see that the frame holds planks? When it rains, the water could push all the sand and mud from their lot. The odd wall keeps their lot where it should be."

"That is just odd," Dave says. "Lil, can you add this bed and truck frame wall to the list?"

They go to the next set of steps. There are 46 steps. The steps go up in a line and do not zigzag. Each step is quite tall. It is like **The Team** must go up a set of tall rungs.

Bade wags his tail, but he wants to be back with Tup. He does not like to be the lead dog up such steep steps.

Jan stops to take a snapshot of pink buds that make a line next to the steps. Tup sniffs at the plants.

At the top of the steps **The Team** all stand still and rest. Jeff is next to his van. He has set up cups of water for all his friends. "Would you like a peach or a plum?" he asks.

"Yes, that would be grand," Lil says. She and three of her friends each have a peach.

Liz's dad takes a big gulp of water. "Have you seen all the gas pipes? They have lots and lots of gas pipes here."

"We have gas pipes in our home," Colt says.

"Yes, but your gas pipes cannot be seen. The gas people had to embed the pipes with sand and sod. Your gas pipes are safe. The gas pipes here can all be seen. They are on top of the land. If they are hit with a truck, they could explode," Liz's dad says.

The kids gaze at the gas pipes. The pipes are next to walls. They are held on homes with clasps and nails.

"That seems unsafe. Should I put that in the odd thing list?" Lil asks.

The kids all nod.

The Step-Up Team goes to the next set of steps and the next. They do not walk so fast. They do not hike up the steps so fast.

They spend lots of time with each sag van. They eat grapes and plums and chips. The dogs drink from water pails in the shade of old trees.

"That is 567 steps," Colt says as he drinks some water. "We are at the top of this hill. Where do we go from here?"

"We walk down this steep street then go to the next set of steps. The one just past that truck," Dave says.

"Wait, do you see that? It is that crate truck we saw when we had a stop on the way into Cactus Gulch," Brad says.

The kids walk fast down the steep hill to get to the load of crates.

1,000 Steps

"Hi," Liz says to the man that stands next to the truck. "It says, 'Home Sweet Home,' on the back of the crates. Is this a small home made to seem like a stack of old crates?"

"No, it is a stack of crates. I get them from shops that had stuff sent to them in the crates. Then I make the crates into things. I make some into puppet stands. Some I make into small homes for kids to play with," the man says.

"That is epic," Quin says. "Can we see the things you make?"

"I have a shop up the street. I will drop this load of crates there, but then I have to go on a trip. I must pick up the next load of crates from shops in the hamlet of Mule Creek. I have to meet the shop people and cannot be late," the man says.

"You can stop at my shop and see into it. You will see what I make. My shop's name is **Joe's Save a Crate Shop**. My name is Joe," the man says.

The kids, moms, and dads tell the man, "Thank you, Joe."

As Joe gets into his truck, Brad says, "May I ask you about the mine? A lot of people said we will be glad we get to go into the mine. Do you know what we will see?"

Joe smiles. "I know, but I cannot say. I can say you will be glad," he says. He waves and drives up the street.

"That was a fine rest. It seems we must wait to know what is in the mine. It is time to get on with our hike," Jan's mom says.

The Step-Up Team is on a street at the base of Cactus Gulch. They walk up to the next set of steps.

There is a wide plank walk way with a hand rail. They must walk on the planks to get to the side of the gulch where the steps are.

"Is this safe?" Colt asks his dad.

"I think this would pass code. The planks are strong and the hand rail does not wag if you shake it. So much in Cactus Gulch is odd. It is odd that it is not odd. It should be on the odd list as it is not odd. It is a plain, strong walk way," Colt's dad says with a smile.

"Just do not jump or run. The hand rail is tall and you could fall into the gulch if you slip," Colt's dad says.

The kids each hold the rail as they cross the planks. They can see the stream rush at the base of the gulch.

There are trees and shrubs next to the stream. Big rocks and small rocks are in the stream.

The water hits the rocks then twists past. They all get to the steps and do not fall into the stream.

"The map says this set of steps has 67 steps," Dave says. He grabs the rail and pulls himself up the steps.

Ms. Jolt stands at the base of the steps. She sniffs the grass. Tup sniffs with her. Bade runs up the steps with Dave. Bade's dog friends want to go with him.

"Hang on, Tup," Jan says. "We do not want you to twist and tie your leash with Ms. Jolt's leash."

The Step-Up Team hikes up the steps. They do not talk so much.

When Brad is up 33 steps he says, "Do you see that home? There is a cactus on top of it. It is in the pipe where the water drains when it rains. Lil, can you add that to the list of odd things?"

"Got it," she says as she jots it down on her notepad.

The Step-Up Team rests at the top of the steps and the next set of steps and the next set.

"There is just one set of steps left," Jan's dad says as they get to the top of some steps.

"Do you see that? It is **Joe's Save a Crate Shop,**" Jan says.

The kids run to the shop. They press next to the glass to see inside.

There are puppet stands, homes for puppets, and play homes that small kids can go into.

The puppet stands have red and white stripes. The puppet homes have names in black and gold. The kids think they could be the names of the puppets.

The homes have lots of shades of paint tints. Some of the paint makes the homes seem like there are plants with pink and red buds next to the homes.

"You would not know they are made from crates," Mave says. "I would like to have some of them to play with. They do not seem odd, but it seems like they should be put on the list as they are so fine."

"Put them on the list," Fran tells Lil. "We can ask Grandpop if he thinks play homes made from crates are odd."

"It is time for our last set of steps," Jan's dad says.

The kids are glad. They want to eat and rest. They are in shock that they are about to reach 1,000 steps.

The last set of steps has lots of trees that make a long shaft-like dome.

The Step-Up Team walks in the shade of the trees. A weak wind makes it so they are not hot. As each of **The Team** steps on the top step, they fill with pride.

They did it! They did a hike of 1,000 steps.

Their friends will gift them cash. They will go to shops and get plush **Read to Me Dogs** for kids. They did the math and know that they will get gifts of $780 plus the cash for the odd stuff they saw. Lots of kids will get plush dogs they can read to.

Liv, Chuck, and Jeff greet **The Team**. They shake their hands. When all of **The Team** is at the top of the steps, Liv's mom says, "We got you a bit of a treat."

Liv, Chuck, and Jeff say at the same time, "PEACH PIE!"

The **Step-Up Team** eats three peach pies. They go back to **The Mules' Bed and Brunch Inn**. They each have a bath then they go out to dine.

They all go to bed and sleep well. When they wake it will be time to go **Into the Mineshaft**. They do not know what they will see in the mine, but they know it will be epic.

Sight Words Used In:
"The Step-Up Team"

a, about, are, as, be, come, comes, could, do, does, down, for, friends, from, go, goes, has, have, he, her, here, hi, his, I, inn, into, is, islands, know, knows, me, Ms., my, no, of, OK, one, onto, or, our, out, people, pull, pulls, push, put, said, saw, says, she, should, so, some, talk, the, their, there, they, to, TVs, two, walk, walks, want, wants, was, water, we, welcome, what, where, would, you, your

Approximately 5,000 words

TRIP TO CACTUS GULCH 2: INTO THE MINESHAFT

Wake Up

Jan wakes up with a cramp in her leg. She does not like it, but she knows what made the cramp happen. She and her friends did a 1,000-Step Hike on the odd and steep steps of Cactus Gulch.

She had times when she did not think she could hike each step. She had times she would think she must stop. Her friends said, "We can do it. Just ten steps to the top." Then they would hold hands and finish the set of steps. Then they would finish the next set and the next set until they got to step 1,000.

The hike was one of the best days in Jan's life. She can tell this day will be just as grand.

The Step-Up Team has plans to go into the Cactus Gulch Mine. The people in Cactus Gulch have said the trip into the mine this day will be epic. They say it will not be like trips in the past, but they will not say what they know.

Jan's dog, Tup, lies next to her on the bed. He licks his leg. Jan thinks he could have a cramp as well. He did the 1,000-Step Hike with her.

"Jan, you are up. So glad to see you this fine day," Jan's dad says.

Gret jumps onto Jan's bed. "Hi sis. You had a long sleep. I went with Mom to get toast and stuff. We will eat at the bench next to the tree with the rest of **The Step-Up Team**."

"That will be yum. I want to eat lots," Jan says.

Gret lays on her back and sticks her legs up. She rubs her feet. "I like that we got to sleep here at **The Mules' Bed and Brunch Inn.** My legs had cramps when we got to the last step. I am glad we did not drive home. The drive home is long. I was in need of lots of sleep."

Gret pulls Jan's blanket on top of her. She says real soft, "Do you know what? Mom and I went and got the mine trip tickets. This way **The Team** will not have to stand in line. You should see the tickets. They are made of brass."

Gret puts her hand in her pants pocket. "They are like the ones real people had when they went to their jobs inside the mine." She pulls out a brass ticket and lets Jan hold it.

"They let you have this?" Jan says. She is in shock that they let Gret have such a grand ticket.

CACTUS GULCH
MINE

67

JOB TAG

She pulls out a brass ticket and lets Jan
hold it.

"Yes. We will have to hand them back when we finish our mine trip. They said that most days they do not let people take the tickets, but this is an epic day so we could take them. We just have to put our names on a list that says which ticket we have."

"Jan, brush your teeth and put on some clean jeans. We can go have brunch with **The Step-Up Team**," Jan's mom says.

All the kids, moms, dads, and three dogs eat brunch next to the trees and fish pond. There are buns, toast, oats, plums, peach jam, pancakes, nuts, muffins, scones, grapes, and lots of stuff.

Most of the 13 kids and 18 moms and dads sit. They all have cramps or just want to rest. They all slept well, but the 1,000-Step Hike left them all spent and beat.

A mule brays from the back lot. "Do you think that is Jonquil or Doe?" Mave asks.

The dogs, Tup, Bade, and Ms. Jolt, run back to see the mules. All the dogs have spent lots of time with colts and oxen so they will not be mean to the mules. They know that big mules can kick. Still, the dads call the dogs back. The dogs should stay here and not go to see the mules.

Jan's mom hands out brass tickets. She jots down each name and which ticket they got. They all pin the tickets to their tops so the tickets do not get lost.

Jeff, Chuck, and Liv had jobs with the sag vans. They gave drinks and snacks to their friends that did the hike.

The three kids did not hike the steps. They do not have leg cramps. They are not beat and spent. They clean up the plates and cups.

Liv cannot walk so she gets from here to there on her seat with wheels. She grabs the plates and such then puts them in bags.

Jeff and Chuck drag the big bags to the trash. If the stuff is plastic or cans, they take it to the bins for Cactus Gulch's **Bring It Back Shop**. They glide their white canes from side to side as they pull the bags on the flagstone. They cannot see and the canes let them know if there is stuff in their path.

The dogs sniff at the bags of trash in hopes they will get a bit to eat. Jeff and Chuck do not rip the bags. The dogs are sad they do not get snacks.

To the Mine

The Step-Up Team grabs their jackets. It will be cold in the mine. The dogs will stay at **The Mules' Bed and Brunch Inn** while **The Team** goes into the mine. The dogs must stay inside so that they do not go to greet the mules or people.

The Team all get into vans and drive to the mine. The kids ask the moms and dads if they know what makes this day so epic. The moms and dads do not know.

"Do you think they will have grand things to eat?" Chuck asks.

"Do you think they will have gifts for people that go into the mine?" Liz asks.

"Do you think they will have bugs that spit flames?" Colt asks.

Colt's mom says, "I hope there are no bugs that spit flames. Hmmm, as I think about it, it would be epic to see a bug spit flames."

"Do you think they will have bugs that spit flames?" Colt asks.

The vans stop and **The Team** gets out. The van lot is next to a big hill. Lots of cactus dot the hill all the way to its top. At the end of the lot there is a tan hut that has **Mineshaft Trip** in red paint on its side.

The Team goes into the hut. Lots and lots of rocks sit on a long shelf that hangs from the wall.

There are old black and white, life-size snapshots of men with mine helmets and mine tops and jeans next to the shelf. The men's clothes are not clean. The men are not clean.

There are snapshots of big, big buckets on wheels. The buckets are so big that six kids could fit in them. The buckets have lots of rocks in them. One snapshot is as big as a life-size mule. It has straps that go back to one of the buckets on wheels.

"Do you see all the dust on the men? They seem to need to rest," Jan says to Gret. "Do you think they broke bones? I bet mine jobs could be unsafe. I bet mine jobs could bring a lot of pain."

Jan's mom hands the gal at the mine the list of names and tickets.

"We will need to check out each ticket at the end of the mine trip, but then you can keep the tickets. We will just do that this day. We want this to be such a big day," the gal says.

"What makes this such a big day?" Jan's mom asks.

The ticket gal smiles but will not say.

The Mine Train

The mine trip can take up to 40 people. **The Step-Up Team** has 31 people. When Jan's mom gave a call to set up this trip two weeks in the past, the mine people said they would just take **The Step-Up Team** into the mine on this trip.

The Team is glad it will just be their friends. That seems like it will be lots of fun.

A man with a mine hat and a lime green vest calls out, "OK, it is time to get set to go into the mineshaft. I need you all to get in a line so we can dress you up."

"Dress us up?" Jeff asks.

"You must each have a mine helmet, a mine lamp, and a green vest like mine," the mine man says.

Chuck and Jeff smile. Jeff says, "We do not need mine lamps. We are blind. The lamps will not help us."

"You must still have a mine lamp," the man says. "The mine is safe, but we still have plans in case a bad thing happens. If the mine's wall lamps go out, it is black in the mine. You must each have a lamp so we can find you."

Jeff nods. "That is a swell plan. I would like you to find me if the wall lamps go out."

The **Step-Up Team** has all their helmets, lamps, and vests. The mine people check that they have their brass tickets.

The Team waits in a line. **The Team** can see out the glass exit. The exit lets in the sunshine. The exit lets them see that there is a small train on tracks.

It is not a big train. It is a get people into the mine train. It has a long seat on each segment of the train.

On the wall next to the line is a black and white snapshot. "That is the train we will ride. See, it is just like the one on the track," Dave says.

"That must be inside the mine," Quin says. "It looks like fun in there."

On the wall next to the line is a black and white snapshot.

The gate into the side of the hill was made so it is just about on top of the train tracks. The train waits on this side of the exit.

The man swings the glass exit out and **The Team** walks to the train.

The Team people each sit on the train seat. Then they swing one leg to cross the seat so that they have a leg on each side of the seat.

Each of the people sits on the seats, then rests their feet on planks on the side of the train.

Liv's dad picks her from her seat with wheels and sets her on the long seat. He sits in back of her. She will lean her back to him if she needs a rest.

Ray and Eve

There will be two mine staff on the mine trip. Ray had a job in a mine one hundred miles from here. He had his job until he got old. He will drive the train. When they are inside the mine, he will tell **The Step-Up Team** tales about this mine.

Eve will ride at the back of the train to keep them safe. Eve's dad is Moe. He had a job in a mine. Moe told Eve lots of tales about his mine job. She knows lots and lots about mines.

"Hi and welcome to all of you," Ray says.

"I had a job in the San Tan mine from when I was 18 until I was 50. I got lots of rocks from the mine. All the rocks got smelt," Ray says.

Ray picks up a rock. "See this rock. There are lots of kinds of rock in this one rock. We do not need all the bits of rock in each rock, we just need some of them," he says.

"To get the bits we need, we smelt the rocks. Smelt means you get the rocks you want and get rid of the kind of rocks you do not want," Ray says. He holds up the rock so **The Team** can see it.

"To smelt the rocks, the mine would roast the rocks to get them hot. They would add flux. The flux would split off the kinds of rocks. It was like the rocks would melt and run like water," Ray says.

"In time, the rocks got put in molds and made into the pipes in your homes. The rocks got smelt and are in your snapshot-tablets and TVs."

"It was a grand job. I have lots of friends still in the mine and we have lots of tales to tell. People that have jobs in mines help make your lives grand."

Ray hands the rock to Jeff's dad so he can pass it to the rest of **The Team**.

"I do want you to think for a bit about what happens when we smelt rocks. It is toxic. It is bad for the land and water. Each time you get a thing made with smelt rocks, toxins have gotten into the land," Ray says.

Jan puts her hand up. "I will take snapshots with my snapshot-tablet while we are here. Rocks got smelt for my tablet. That means I made the land toxic? I do not like that."

Ray nods. "Then I want you to think about this. You should read lots and lots. You should do lots of math. You should get to know so much that you can think up fresh ways to make stuff."

Ray gets the rock from Jan's mom and sets it on a shelf.

"You should think up fresh ways to smelt rocks. Then when you are big you can get jobs that find ways to make pipes and snapshot-tablets that are not toxic. You kids can do a lot to come up with fresh ways that are not toxic," Ray says.

Ray smiles at Jan. "I do not mean to make you sad. I just want you kids to know it is time for you to think up fresh plans. I know you will."

"Ray, do you want to tell them that this mine trip is not like mine trips in the past?" Eve asks.

"Yes, can you please tell us that?" Jeff asks.

Ray smiles. "This mine trip will be epic. The people of Cactus Gulch had a vote. We set this date as the date for it to happen. That is all I will say about that."

He goes to the gate in the hill. He swings the gate out so that it is not shut.

The Team can see into the mineshaft in the side of the hill. The tracks can be seen a bit, the mineshaft walls can be seen a bit. Then it is all black.

Ray flips a tab and a line of wall lamps comes on.

"It is time to go into the mineshaft," Ray says.

150 Feet

Ray sits on his seat. He makes the train go. It stops then goes then stops then goes. It shakes as the wheels click on the track. It does not go fast, but it does shake.

Ray stops the train and gets off his seat. Eve gets off her seat and walks back and shuts the exit gate.

"We are 150 feet into the mine. Take a bit of time to see if you are OK. Some people do not like to be in mines. If you want to go out, Eve will take you."

Ray walks up and down the side of the train. **The Step-Up Team** is fine. Ray and Eve go back to their seats.

"What do you see in here?" Chuck asks Colt.

"The top of the shaft is a bit like a long dome. The walls and top are rock. The track sits on flat land. There are wall lamps; about one each 20 feet. It seems dim, but we can see just fine. There is a shaft with vents at the top. I think that brings in fresh wind," Colt says.

"They shut the exit. I could tell. What was that for?" Chuck asks.

"It helps the vents do their job," Eve says. "A fan makes the wind in the shaft. If we did not shut the exit, the wind would suck out and it would not be fresh in here."

"Are you all set to go?" Ray asks.

The Step-Up Team nod and say, "Yes."

Ray makes the train go. It stops then goes then stops then goes. It shakes as the wheels click on the track. Then he brings it to a stop.

Plank Steps and Walls

There is a set of steps made from planks. The walls next to the steps have planks. The rails they grab with their hands are made of pipes.

The Step-Up Team hike up the steps. Most think their legs would like to rest.

Chuck and Jeff have their canes, but their moms help them so they do not trip as they step on the plank steps. Liv's dad has a backpack that Liv's mom made. Liv sits in it and rides on her dad's back.

The Team is at the top of the steps. There is a deck made from planks. Most of the sides of the deck are rock. One side has a plank wall that is about three feet tall.

The Team stands next to the small wall. They can see down into the mine. It is like a big cave. There are wall lamps down there so it is not black.

"Let me tell you about this mine. It is old. They shut it down two decades in the past. They got all the rocks they could smelt. The rocks you see would not do well in the smelt so they made it for people to do trips like ours. Until they shut it, they got lots of rocks from here," Ray says.

Ray puts his hand on the mine wall. "It was a cave way back 14 decades in the past. The men came in a cave hole that is down that way. They would step down rungs. They would bring buckets and rods to tap into the rocks. They did not have lamps like we do. They had wax with wicks and flames to see."

Ray holds up a steel rod. "One man would hold a tap rod to the rock wall. His pal would hit it to crush the rock. They would put the rocks in the buckets and take them up the rungs with them," Ray says.

"Did they hit their hands?" Mave asks.

Ray nods. "They did. Some broke their bones. They would bind their hands with tape and get back to their job. If they did not crush rock, they did not get their pay."

"You see all the planks here?" Ray waves at the deck and steps. "There came a time when they did an update to the mine."

"It was a big thing when they put tracks for the mule train into the mine. When they had the mule train, they could take out lots of rock. That is when they made blasts to explode the rocks. They would take the big piles of rocks and put them in train buckets," Ray says.

"If the blast had a problem, it could make the mine fall and crush the men. They held up the mine with big planks and beams made from soft trees. The planks would squeak and groan and shift if the mine was set to crash down. If the planks gave groans, the men would run out so they could be safe," Ray says.

"Did men die in here?" Jan asks.

"Yes.   About   two hundred men did die," Ray says.

Jan is sad. "Just so I could have my snapshot-tablet?"

Ray shrugs. "They did not have snapshot-tablets back when this mine had the best rocks. The mines could be unsafe back then. These days, mines are safe. My friends that still have jobs in mines feel safe."

Jan is glad about that.

"There is a snapshot of a mule in the mine hut. The name of the inn we slept at is 'The Mules'. You said they put in mule trains. Can you tell us about the mules?" Liz asks.

"They had mules to pull the train buckets. The rocks would go in the buckets and the mules would pull them to the exits," Ray says.

"The mules did not go out of the mines. The mules each had to stay in the mine for 1,460 days. They had to be in the mine so long and did not get to see sunshine. That long with no sunshine made it so they could not see," Ray says.

The kids all gasp.

"It is OK. At the end of the mules' days in the mine, the people would put a blindfold on the mules and lead them out of the mine. They had to have the blindfold on or the sun would blind them," Ray says.

"When they got up on the land, the mule men would poke holes in the blindfold. Just one or two holes each two or three days. The mule would see just spots of sunshine. Then they would see the next one or two spots of sunshine. In 4 or 5 weeks, they would take off the blindfold and the mule could see," Ray says.

"Then it would get sold to a ranch where it could have a job in the sunshine for the rest of its life," Ray says.

"Do you know that the mules had fun in here? They made friends with all the men. They would lean next to them so the men would pet them. They would steal a sandwich or a plum. The men and mules had fun," Ray says.

Ray walks to the steps. "Let us get on the train. I will take you to see the drills."

Mine Drills

The Step-Up Team gets on the train then goes deep into the mine.

There is a big plank with red paint that says, "Stop," in white paint. It hangs down next to the train.

This stop does not have steps. There is a path off to the side of the tracks. **The Team** goes with Ray on the path.

There is a big thing with three legs. It seems to be made of steel. It is long and has handgrips you could hold onto.

"This is a mine drill," Ray says. "It let the men drill holes for blasts. It is so big two men had to hold it. They would drill a bunch of holes, put in blast sticks, then walk up the mine where they would be safe. They did not run. If they ran, they could trip then die in the blast."

Chuck's dad helps Chuck feel the drill with his hands. "I bet the drills gave a lot of help," Chuck says.

"Yes, they got a lot of holes made with them. The down side was they made lots of dust. The dust would get in the men's lungs and they would die when they got to be about 40," Ray says.

"That is so sad," Fran says.

"Real sad. The men's wives and kids would be left with no dad," Ray says. "Then they got drills that had water. It kept the dust down. The men did not die from the dust."

Ray walks up a bit on the path. There is a small drill. "This drill is not so big. One man could hold it. He would drill holes then put in blast sticks. He would put in blast wicks. Some wicks would be not so long, some would be real long. The size of the blast wick would say when they would explode."

"There was a way to have the blast sticks explode to get the best holes. The wicks would be lit with a flame. The man would walk up the path. The mine wall would explode. The next day, he and his pals would lift the rock into the train buckets and the mules would pull the rock out of the mine."

Fran sees a line of rock with a tint that is not like the rest of the rock. She scans the walls and sees lines that are not the same tint as the rest. "Can you please tell me about all the lines in the rocks?"

Ray smiles at Eve. Eve smiles back. "That is a grand thing you ask," Ray says.

Jan thinks their smiles are odd. She wants to know if it has to do with the epic thing that is to happen.

Ray puts his hand on a line in the rock. "There are lots of kinds of rocks in the hills. There are hundreds of kinds of rocks in the hills next to Cactus Gulch."

"There are the ones we smelt, there is gold, there is fake gold," Ray says.

"Did you know that fake gold can ignite into flames?" Ray says.

"The rocks would ignite? That is odd," Jeff says.

"There is a mine in a state back east that has had flames for about six decades. If there is lots of rock, there can be lots of flames," Ray says.

"I saw you smile at Eve," Jan says. "Can you tell us about your smiles? Are they about the epic thing we will see?" Jan asks.

Ray smiles at Jan. "Would you like to know what you will see?" he asks.

"Yes," **The Step-Up Team** says.

The Vote

Eve stands next to Ray. "The people of Cactus Gulch know all about this mine."

Ray nods. "Yes, we do."

Eve says, "When the sun has set, we will all come here for picnics. We go for walks and make the train go real fast."

"We bring Jonquil and Doe in here so they can bray like the mules from the past," Ray says.

"We have seen things in the mine that people that come here for mine trips have not seen," Eve says.

"Will we see an elf?" Mave asks.

"An elf? That would be grand," Eve says. "Come, let us get back on the train. And do not run. Do as the men from the past did, walk to the train. Do not run so you do not trip."

The Step-Up Team gets back to their seats on the train. Eve and Ray stand next to the train.

"**The Old People** of Cactus Gulch said they would like to have a talk. They said they want the public to know. They said they know life will not be the same if we tell the public," Eve says.

"All the people of Cactus Gulch had a vote. Did we want the public to know or not?" Eve says.

"Know what?" Colt says.

"I will get to that," Eve says.

"If we told the public, they would all want to see. There would be lots and lots of people come to the mine. It could be **The Old People** would be sad. It could be they wish we did not tell the public," Eve says.

Jan cannot think what Eve means.

"If we did not tell the public, then it would stay hidden. We did a vote and the people of Cactus Gulch said that it is so grand we do not want it hidden. **The Old People** are keen and bold. We said that their lives would not be the same. They said that is OK," Ray says.

"What is hidden? What is grand?" Chuck asks.

"Hang on. You will see," Ray says.

Ray flips a tab and a long line of wall lamps shine in the mineshaft. Ray and Eve get to their seats. Ray makes the train go. It stops then goes then stops then goes. It shakes as the wheels click on the track.

The train goes and goes. It goes a long way. Ray brings the train to a stop. He gets off his seat.

"We did not want to put this online. We did not want to tell the press about this. **The Old People** said this is the way the want us to do this. They said to have a vote," Eve says.

"So, the people of Cactus Gulch had a vote. We all said it would be best to just bring people here. Please, come with me," Ray says as he walks into the mineshaft.

The **Step-Up Team** get off the train and go with him. There is a big hole in the wall into a cave. **The Team** steps into the cave. The cave is lit with bits of sunshine that seep from cracks at the top of the cave.

"Gosh," Jan says.

Gret takes Jan's hand. "This is epic," Gret says.

"I have not seen a cave like this," Colt's dad says.

"I am in shock," Liv's mom says.

"What is it? What is it?" Jeff and Chuck ask.

"It is what the hills made a long time in the past," Ray says.

"I have not seen a cave like this," Colt's dad says.

"It is a stone cave," Jeff's mom says. "It is big. It is about the size of the lots where people play ballgames. There are stones that seem like they could be glass."

"There are green rocks and white rocks. There are rocks like the waves on an island beach," Chuck's mom says.

"The glass rocks are the best," Fran says. "It is like they are strands of glass. Some are two feet long. Some hang from the top of the cave."

"This is so epic," Jan says.

Then a man talks.

The Old People

"Welcome to our home," a man says.

The Step-Up Team gazes here and there. They do not see the man.

"I am not tall," the man says. "Well, my friends think I am tall. You will not think that."

There is a scruff and a drag from next to a big green rock. Jan thinks she sees what could be a red dog. It is not a red dog. A red reptile with a long neck and spikes on its back comes out from next to the rock.

"What kind of reptile is that?" Colt asks.

"A reptile? Here in the mine?" Jeff asks.

"No, in the cave. There is a small man on its back," Colt says.

"The reptile is a geck," Ray says.

The Step-Up Team does not know what to think or say or do. The man has green skin. He has pink braids. He has on a kilt. There are teal wings on his back.

The man's reptile walks to a wax stick. The geck pucks his lips and flames come out. The flames lick the tips of the wax sticks and they each flush with flames.

When there is a small line of flames, the reptile and man come up to **The Step-Up Team**.

"Welcome to our home," the man says. "I am Devin. We are glad you came to see us. We do not want to be hidden. We want the public to know we are here."

A bunch of reptiles come out to be seen. The gecks are green, red, pink, plum, teal, and white. On each reptile's back is a man, gal, or child. The people all have green skin, pink braids, and teal wings. They all have kilts on.

"Are you **The Hill People**?" Colt and Mave's dad asks.

"No, **The Hill People** had black braids and tan skin. They had to go. They left Cactus Gulch when their big people left ten decades in the past. They had to go to help their big people. That was a sad time in the past," Devin the green man says.

"We are **The Old People**. **The Hill People** came to us with an ask. They said they would like us to do their job until they can come back. We are here to help the hills and the caves. We will be glad when **The Hill People** come back. They are keen and bold," Devin says as he sits on his red geck.

"It is about time for the vines," a green gal with a gold top says.

The cave hums. **The Step-Up Team** gazes here and there. From the top crack in the cave a ray of sun beams down into the cave. The ray gets big. It is like lots and lots of lamps shine from the top of the cave.

A ray of sun shines on a glass rock. It shakes and hums. The next rock hums as does the next rock and the next. The rocks sing a sweet song.

"They are here. The vines and buds are here," a child with small wings says.

A vine creeps on the base of the cave. A leaf pops from the vine's stem. Then there is a leaf that pops just down the stem. The pop, pop, pop, of each leaf fills the cave.

There is a sweet smell and buds come out of each leaf. Most buds are white, but some are pink.

The Old People flap their wings and drift up from their reptiles. They go to the buds and drink from them.

The cave is full of vines and buds. **The Old People** flit from one bud to the next. The song of the rocks is a glad song. The smell of the buds is like the smell of rain on cactus.

The sunshine gets a bit dim, then the last ray of sun goes from the rocks. The rocks are still and their song stops. Each leaf goes back into the vine then the vine pulls back to hide within the rocks. The line of wax sticks flame and shine into the cave.

The Step-Up Team does not say a thing. They are in shock. They are all glad for what they saw.

In a bit, Colt and Mave's dad says, "I have elf-friends. I have seen a thing or two, but I have not seen a thing like that. Did that happen? Did I see that?"

Devin, the green man with teal wings nods. "Yes, you came on the best trip of the day. That happens just one time each day when the sun is on top of the cave's crack. You came for our lunchtime," the man says.

"When the sun shines into the cave the buds let us eat. The song is from the sonic waves as the rocks shake from the heat of the sun. The next trip of **Big People** will not get to see that, they will just get to meet us," a green gal says.

"Are we **Big People**?" Liz asks.

Devin nods.

"If they get to meet you, they will think that is grand," Liv says.

"If you are not **The Hill People**, where do you come from?" Mave's dad asks.

"We are from the caves next to a sea. That is a long way from here. We came to help. This is our home until **The Hill People** come back," Devin says.

"We have seen the public on TV. We want to get to know you. **The Big People** of Cactus Gulch are kind and fun. We think it is a grand plan if the rest of your people know we are here," the gal with the gold top says.

The Way Back

Time seems to go so fast for **The Step-Up Team**. It is time they must get back to the train and go out from the mine.

Devin rides his reptile up to Quin and Dave. He says, "The Grump Grunt told me you would be here. He is my friend. He said you are his friends. He thinks you would like the clock. Do you have a notepad that you can jot down on?"

"I have a notepad," Lil says.

"Then I will spell this for you. You can have your mom or dad read it when you get out of the mine. Please jot down 'r-e-w-i-n-d c-l-o-c-k.' If you go to the shops in Cactus Gulch, you will find that clock," Devin says.

Lil jots it down, then rips the note from her notepad and hands it to Dave.

"Thank you," Dave tells the green man.

The Team gets on the train and Ray makes the train go. It stops then goes then stops then goes. It shakes as the wheels click on the track.

The Team gets back to the mine hut. They must take off their mine helmets and lime green vests.

They lay their mine lamps down so that the next set of people can have them.

They hand their brass tickets to the ticket gal. She checks them off the list and hands them back their tickets. They are all glad they get to keep the brass tickets.

The next people stand in a line. A small child walks up to Jan. "I was told this trip would be epic. I was told what we see will be grand. Was your trip epic?"

Jan nods. "It was the most epic trip. You have grand luck that you will get to see it."

"What is it?" the child's mom says.

"It is a hidden and it is grand," Jan's mom says. "That is all we will say."

The Step-Up Team goes to their vans.

"That was epic," Jan says.

Sight Words Used In:
"Into the Mineshaft"

a, about, are, as, be, come, comes, could, do, does, down, for, friends, from, full, go, goes, have, he, her, here, hi, his, Hmmm, I, inn, into, is, island, know, knows, me, Ms., my, no, of, one, ones, onto, or, our, ours, out, people, please, pull, pulls, put, puts, said, saw, she, should, so, some, talk, talks, the, their, there, they, to, TV, TVs, two, was, water, we, welcome, where, would, you, your

Approximately 6,000 words

PLAY THE BAGPIPES

The Way to Class

Steve and Delsin are friends. They take a **Bake It** class at **The Make It, Bake It, and Taste It Muffin and Scone Shop**.

The class is up the street from Delsin's home.

The two friends walk from Delsin's home past the play land to the **Bake it Shop**. The play land has swings and slides.

The play land has a hill. As they walk, Steve and Delsin see a man on the hill. The man holds a cloth bag with sticks.

The man hugs the bag and puffs into one of the sticks. His hand slides and taps on a stick that hangs down from the bag. The bag makes a grand song. It is a song that makes them think of a long-lost land.

A man in a dress made a bag and sticks play a song.

When they get to the **Bake It Class**, Steve tells Ms. Hamlet, "A man in a dress made a bag and sticks play a song. It was a grand song."

Ms. Hamlet says, "I see that man when I come to my shop."

She lifts a muffin tin from her cloth bag. "He plays the bagpipes. That is not a dress, it is a kilt."

"Men in Scotland have kilts. Lots of people that play bagpipes have kilts. When they meet to play as a club, they all have their kilts. It is a grand thing to see," Ms. Hamlet says.

Steve

Steve is at lunch with his mom and dad, "May I get a set of bagpipes? I would like to play the bagpipes," Steve says.

"Bagpipes are fine for hilltops. We do not have a hilltop. Up close and inside they squeak and yell," his dad says.

Steve's mom sets down her glass of tea. "If you got bagpipes the people up and down our street would call us," she says.

She sips her tea. "They would ask if our cat is in pain. They would say, 'Did your cat get its tail stuck in the trashcan lid?' We would have to say, 'No, that is Steve and his bagpipes.'"

Steve does not bite his sandwich. "What if I play the bagpipes in our back lot? People could see it was me. They would not think it was our cat," Steve says. "Our cat stays inside. They would not think it was our cat."

Steve's dad smiles. "If you got bagpipes our cat would make an epic yell. The yell would go up and down the street. People would think the cat is in pain when you play the bagpipes," he says.

"What if we get you a drum? I bet Mr. Ling would teach you to play the drum," Steve's dad has a bite of green beans.

I bet Mr. Ling would teach you to play the drum

Steve's mom twists her lips like she cannot think of what to say.

"Bagpipes would upset the cat. Would you like a trumpet or a trombone? There are lots of fine things you can play that do not screech like a bagpipe. There are lots of things you can play that would not upset our cat."

Delsin

Delsin did not ask his mom if he could get a bagpipe. He did not ask his dad if he can get bagpipes.

Delsin's home does not have a lot. His home is at the top of a tall, tall complex.

Delsin's mom says they have a quaint walk-up. His dad says they have a flat. Delsin just calls it home.

Delsin must ride in a lift to get up to his home. Then he walks in a long hall with green walls. Lots of moms and dads with kids rent flats in this hall.

In the flat next to Delsin's, there is a man. He just came to the complex in the last two weeks. Delsin does not see him much.

When Delsin walks pass the man's flat he smells relish.

Delsin does not like relish. He does not like to inhale the smell. When lunch is a sandwich with relish, he wipes off the relish.

When Delsin thinks where he could play a bagpipe, the complex lift comes to mind. He could be in the lift just himself. He could play the bagpipes in the lift.

Then he thinks of Ms. Reach. Her flat is next to the lift. Her job is to help people that are sick.

When he sleeps, she is at her job. When he would play the bagpipes is when she sleeps. She would be upset if his bagpipes did not let her sleep. He does not want to do that to her.

Bake It Class

Delsin is glad Steve is in his **Bake It Class**. They are a **Bake It Team**.

They made a pumpkin twist with a sweet glaze. Then they made a wheat loaf with nuts and seeds.

Then they made a wheat loaf with nuts and seeds.

Delsin got to take his treats home to his mom. She said if he got a list of the stuff in it, she would help him make it at home.

It is their last class. The class test is to make peach muffins with nutmeg.

Steve reads from the volume, **Bake the Best Muffins**. Delsin does what Steve reads for him to do.

"Whip the egg with the whisk." Then he says, "Sift the wheat then chop the peach." At the end, Steve says, "To finish them, you dust with the nutmeg and sweet stuff."

Steve does not whip, sift, or dust. He did that last week when Steve said what **Bake the Best Scones** said to do.

In class, Delsin does all the steps to mix the peach muffins. Then he sets the muffin pan on the rack so they can bake. As they get hot, he can smell them. The smell is YUM! He cannot wait to taste them.

"It is time to check the muffins," Ms. Hamlet says.

Delsin gets a set of hotmitts. He puts one on each of his hands. He gets the muffin pan from the rack and sets it on a stand. The smell is so yum.

"When they are not so hot, you can taste them," Ms. Hamlet says.

When the muffins are not so hot, Steve has a bite. "You did a fine job. I like your muffins," he tells Delsin.

At Delsin's Complex

At his complex, Delsin gets on the lift. He has a box of muffins in his backpack. He goes up and up and up until the lift comes to a stop.

Delsin walks up the hall. He sees the man in the flat next to his. He is in the hall with a basket of plums and grapes.

He sees the man in the flat next to his. He is in the hall with a basket of plums and grapes.

"Hi," says the man.

"Hi," Delsin says. "Would you like a muffin? I made them. I had a bit of help from a friend, but I got to whip, sift, and dust them."

"Yes, I would like a muffin," the man says.

Delsin holds the muffin box and the man gets out a big muffin. He takes a bite. "This is a fine muffin. I like it. You bake well."

Delsin smiles. He is glad the man said he can bake well. "What is the basket of plums and grapes for?" he asks the man.

"I will go to the ranch where Calvin and Dublin are at. I do not see them all the time, so when I go, I take snacks," the man says.

"A ranch? You go to a ranch? Are Calvin and Dublin your colts?" Delsin asks. "Will you give them the plums and grapes?"

"No, I do not have colts. The ranch does not have colts. Calvin and Dublin are oxen. The snacks are for my friend Dennis Hamlet and his wife," the man says. He takes a bite of muffin.

Delsin is in shock. "Dennis Hamlet? Is his wife Robin Hamlet? Ms. Hamlet has the **Bake Shop**. I go there so she can teach me to bake."

"Well, yes, Robin Hamlet is his wife. Would you like to come to their ranch?" the man says.

"Ask your mom and dad if they can bring you. You can meet Calvin and Dublin," the man says.

"We have not met. I spend most of my time at my job or at the Hamlet Ranch. Dennis Hamlet is the man I see to teach me the ways to plant stuff. I till the land and plant seeds then I go to my job," the man says as he takes a bite of muffin.

I till the land and plant seeds
then I go to my job.

"I come home late. All I want to do is sleep so I make a sandwich to eat and read in bed. Then I sleep and get up to go to the Hamlet Ranch. My name is Edmund Congress," the man says. He holds out his hand for Delsin.

"I am glad to meet you Mr. Congress. My name is Delsin," Delsin says. He shakes the man's hand.

"Just call me Ed. I have a long name so Ed is best," Ed says. "Have your mom or dad come see me. We can make plans for them to bring you to the Hamlet Ranch."

"Will it be OK with Mr. and Ms. Hamlet if I come to their ranch?" Delsin says.

"I will ask them, but I think they will say yes. My friend Jazmin and her kid Liz spend lots of time there. Jazmin's sis Jill and her sis Jean bring their kids as well. There can be lots of cousins there from time to time. I would think they would be glad to meet you," Ed says.

"Do you think I could invite my friend Steve? He likes Ms. Hamlet. I bet he would like to meet some oxen," Delsin says.

"I will ask her if it is OK. I bet it will be," Ed says.

The Cop

Delsin and Steve are in the back of Delsin's van. Delsin's mom and dad each said they would like to go see the oxen so they all drive there.

Steve's mom and dad each had to go to their jobs. They will meet the oxen some time when it is their time to drive.

Ed leans on the oxen gate. Dennis Hamlet and Robin Hamlet are with him. They all wave when Delsin's van pulls up and stops.

Steve gets out of the van. "We have met," he says to Ed.

Ed squints to see Steve. "Yes, we have. You and your mom gave 911 a call when the spring fell in the lane."

"A spring in the lane? Did a big pipe have a leak?" Dennis Hamlet says.

"No. It was a big spring that fell off a truck. It was made from steel. It was 12 feet tall," Ed says.

Steve shakes Ed's hand. "Ms. Hamlet, this is the cop that came to help with the spring in the lane. He got them to send a crane to take it out of the street. He set up cones and tape next to the spring so people would not hit it," Steve says.

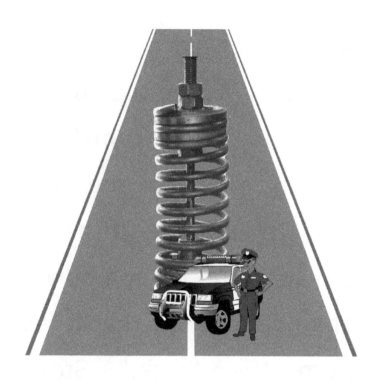

Ms. Hamlet, this is the cop that came to help with the spring in the lane.

"That is epic," Delsin says. "You did not tell me this tale. Where did such a big spring come from?"

"It was for the sun scope they made. It makes the scope go up and down. They did not see that it fell from the truck," Steve says.

"It was that big and they did not see it fall from the truck?" Dennis Hamlet says.

Ed shrugs. "It was on the back of their truck. They may have had to rush to get there on time. When people rush, they can miss stuff," he says.

"Well, to miss a 12 feet tall steel spring that falls from your truck is quite a shock," Delsin says.

They all smile.

Dennis Hamlet waves to the oxen in the lot. "Come meet Calvin and Dublin. They like when people pet them."

Steve, Delsin, and all the rest go to the gate. Dennis Hamlet swings the gate and they all walk into the lot. Calvin and Dublin walk up to the bunch of people.

The oxen's tails hang down like lines. "See their tails?" Dennis Hamlet says. "That means they are glad to meet you."

Steve and Delsin pet the oxen.

"This is epic," Delsin says.

Robin Hamlet brings out some muffins and scones. Delsin's mom and dad and Ed each take one muffin.

Robin Hamlet says to the kids, "You can each have two." Steve and Delsin smile. Robin Hamlet bakes the best muffins they have had.

Time to Go

Dennis Hamlet takes them to his back lot where he plants seeds.

The green plants reach for the sun. The plants are all in lines. Dennis Hamlet takes pride in his lines of plants. He says that Calvin and Dublin help him till the land.

Delsin's mom and dad ask Dennis Hamlet lots and lots. When they do not have things left to ask, they go back to see Calvin and Dublin.

"You are welcome to stay with the oxen," Dennis Hamlet says. "Ed and I must go. It is time for us to play our bagpipes."

"You play bagpipes?" Steve and Delsin say at the same time.

"Yes, we have a bagpipe band," Ed says.

"Where does your bagpipe band play?" Delsin asks.

"We play at ballgames and truck sales lots. We play when lots of Scottish people have meet and greets," Ed says.

"Yes, we have a bagpipe band," Ed says.

"We play at lots and lots of things. The one time we do not play is if it is inside," Dennis Hamlet says.

"That is a fine plan," Delsin's mom says. "I bet bagpipes inside would be bad."

Dennis Hamlet nods. "Yes. When we play inside, we get calls that ask if our cat is OK."

"Dennis Hamlet, Delsin and I would like to play the bagpipes. Our moms and dads will not let us play. They said bagpipes would upset the people on our street. Where could we play bagpipes?" Steve asks.

"It takes a long time to play the bagpipes well," Dennis Hamlet says. "You can play at your home if you like."

"No, he cannot play the bagpipes at our home. We have a flat in a complex. The people there will not like it if Delsin plays the bagpipes," Delsin's mom says.

"You do not get a bagpipe for a long time. I could teach him to play the Teach Stick. That is what I call it, but most people do not call it that. The Teach Stick is small and does not screech like a cat in pain," Dennis Hamlet says.

The Teach Stick is small and does not screech like a cat in pain.

"Please Mom, may I? We could ask Steve's mom if he can get a Teach Stick," Delsin says.

"That could be OK," Delsin's mom says. "I have one thing I would like to ask, if I may," she says to Dennis Hamlet.

Dennis Hamlet nods. "What would you like to ask?"

"Where would they play when they are set for bagpipes? I do not want to upset the people in our complex," Delsin's mom says.

"They could come here," Dennis Hamlet says.

"We play to the plants and oxen. I think it makes the plants get real tall and strong. The oxen do not mind. Well, they do not mind as long as they get some oats while we play," Dennis Hamlet says.

"Then Delsin, I will let Dennis Hamlet teach you to play the bagpipes. Steve, I will ask your mom if you can play as well."

"That is just grand," Robin Hamlet says. She claps her hands.

Delsin and Steve smile. Each is glad they will get to play the bagpipes.

The End

The real name for a "teach stick" is the Practice Chanter.

Sight Words Used In:
"Play the Bagpipes"

a, are, as, be, come, comes, could, cousins, do, does, down, for, friend, friends, from, go, goes, has, have, he, her, here, hi, his, I, into, is, me, Mr., Ms., my, no, of, OK, one, or, our, out, people, please, pulls, puts, said, says, she, so, some, the, their, there, they, to, two, was, we, welcome, what, where, would, you, your

Approximately 2,500 words

THE HIDDEN TALE 1:
THE LOST SNAPSHOT

What Will They Find?

Lil and Liz are cousins. They hold hands with their cousin Jeff and his friend Chuck. The kids run up the steps of **The Public Hall for Tomes of Tales**.

The 4 kids do not know that, in just a bit, they will find the lost snapshot. They do not know that they are about to seek out **The Hidden Tale**.

The Public Hall

As they run up the steps of **The Public Hall**, Jeff and Chuck trust that Lil and Liz will keep them safe. They will not let them trip and fall.

Liz's mom, Jazmin, runs to keep up with them.

"You kids are way fast. Wait up," Jazmin calls with a smile.

"But Mom, Lil wants to see her mom," Liz calls back.

The kids get to the top step. Lil and Liz gaze up at the tall stone walls of **The Public Hall**.

The kids do not go inside. They must wait for Liz's mom. She has the white canes that Jeff and Chuck hold when they walk. They cannot see so they must hold canes if they do not hold a friend's hand.

Lil's mom is Jill. Jill's job is in **The Public Hall for Tomes of Tales**. Lil stays with Liz and her Aunt Jazmin while Jill goes to her job.

Jill helps people find what they want to read. **The Public Hall** has so much stuff to read. There are volumes and volumes on shelf upon shelf.

The Public Hall has laptops on island desks where people can list what they want to find.

The laptop will flash on its screen, "You can find that on the kids' shelf." It could say, "You can find stuff to read about dogs on the pet shelf."

The laptop could say, "We do not have volumes that will teach you to bake **Stuff in Crust**. Please ask our staff to help you find that."

When the laptop cannot help people find what they want to read, they seek out Jill.

Jill will smile and say, "May I help you?" Then she gets out the old index file box that lists old, old volumes that are not on the laptop lists. She has lots of fun when she can help people.

A Plant for Oxen

Jill sees Lil. She smiles. "Hi, my sweets."

Lil runs to her mom and they hug.

"Hi, sis," Jill says to Jazmin. Jill smiles at Liz, Jeff, and Chuck. "Hi kids. I am glad you could all come see me. Liz, you got braids. They are so cute."

Liz smiles. She is glad to see her aunt. "Mom put in the braids. I had to hold still while she did it."

"Well, they are sweet. What brings you here?" Jill asks.

"Aunt Jazmin wants to read about sick oxen," Jeff says.

"Sick oxen?" Jill squints. "Are Anvil or Magnet sick? They are old oxen. I will be upset if they are sick."

"No, Anvil and Magnet are in tiptop shape. I want to read about which plants could be tonics if they get sick. It would be best if I could get plants that keep them well," Jazmin says.

"Mom says we have a small plot of land in back of our home. She thinks it would be a fine plan to put in plants to keep the oxen well," Liz says.

Jill nods. "Yes, that is a fine plan. You are kind to want to keep them well."

"Mom, can you think what we had for lunch?" Lil says.

"Did you go to **The Make It, Bake It, and Taste It Muffin and Scone Shop**?" Jill asks.

"Nope. **The Five and Dime**," Liz says.

"Then you must have had a sandwich and spuds," Jill says.

"And a cut up peach with nut cream," Lil tells her mom.

"I did not have a sandwich," Chuck says. "I had **Toad on Toast**."

Jill squints. "**Toad on Toast** is yum, but I cannot eat it. That name makes me think of my pet frog Handspring."

"Mom, you had Handspring as a child. You said he had a long frog life," Lil says.

"Yes, he did. He was a grand frog. I got him as a tadpole. When he got all his legs, he was so big he went to Mr. Ling's. He spent his life in Mr. Ling's fish and frog pond," Jill says.

"Handspring would do flips in his pond when Mom went to see him" Lil says.

"*Handspring would do flips in his pond when Mom went to see him*" Lil says.

"I still miss him," Jill says. She seems a bit sad, then she smiles. "Did you like the **Toad on Toast**?" she asks Chuck.

"Yes. I had beans and kale. I did not want cream on top," Chuck says.

"Let us tell Jill about lunch when she gets home. She has a job to do and I need her help. So, Jill, can you help me find if there is a leaf or plant that would keep the oxen well? I did a seek and find on the laptop and it said to ask you," Jazmin says.

Jill nods. "There are lots of old vet, medic, and ranch things in the index that you cannot find on the laptop. We need to update our laptop files with the old, classic volumes. I would think we will find lots of ranch tips in the index," she says as she lifts the lid on the index box.

Jill flips from file to file as she seeks a note about plants that keep oxen well. She comes to a stop and reads. "Nope, not that one." She flips and flips then stops. "Nope." She flips and stops and says, "Here, this could be what you want." She holds up the file for her sis to read.

Jazmin nods as she reads. "Yes, this could do the job. The name is **'Like Catnip for Oxen: The Leaf that will help your Oxen and Livestock Reach Wellness in Their Olden Golden Days.'** This says the filmstrip was made at the **Quail Spring Ranch**. That was close to here a long time in the past, I think."

Jill smiles. "Yes, it was. That is where **The Ping Pang Gas Shop** and **The Dog Wog Pet Shop** are. That filmstrip must be quite old." Jill jots down the name of the filmstrip and 636.

"What is six-three-six?" Jazmin asks.

"That is the shelf where you can find this filmstrip. It is in the basement with all the old and classic stuff," Jill says.

Jazmin takes the note from her sis. She and the kids go down the steps into the basement to find the filmstrip.

The Basement

Liz and Lil hop and jump down the steps. Jeff and Chuck hold the hand rail to lead them down the steps. They all stop half way down. "It stinks. What is that smell?" Jeff asks.

Lil sniffs. "It is dank. It smells like Mr. Ling's fish shed. That is odd. His shed is dank from all the water. I cannot think what makes it smell dank down here."

Jazmin steps next to the kids. "There could be a leak in the pipes. We should tell Jill when we go up the steps. There could be mold in the walls."

Lil and Liz squint to see in the unlit basement. Jazmin flips a tab. A bulb in a socket hangs from the top of the basement. It helps them see just a bit.

The basement has shelf upon shelf. Each shelf has volume upon volume or box upon box. Each box and each volume have a film of dust.

A bulb in a socket hangs from the top of the basement. It helps them see just a bit.

There is so much stuff on each shelf that it seems they could fall and crash.

As they finish their trip down the steps, puffs of dust come up and coat their flip flops. At the back of the basement is a big red EXIT at the top of the wall. "It says 'exit.' That must be a way to get out," Liz tells Jeff.

"It is dank. There is so much dust. I cannot see much. It smells of mold and dust. This is an odd basement. I am glad there is a back way out," Lil says.

Jazmin goes to the shelf that says 636. She reads each filmstrip box.

"Mom," Liz says, "What is a filmstrip?"

"That is what kids in class got to see a long time in the past. They did not invent laptops back then. A class would not have a TV to see films," Jazmin says as she peeks at each box.

"A filmstrip is a long film that has lots of snapshots. The snapshots shine on a white screen. You see one snapshot at a time," Jazmin says as she reads a box.

"The gal or man that leads the class plays a tape at the same time. People would talk on the tape. They would say stuff about the snapshot. Then there would be a dong and it would be time to see the next snapshot," Jazmin says as she checks this shelf and the next shelf.

"Here it is," Jazmin says. She takes the filmstrip box from the shelf.

The kids go to Jazmin to find out what she has. Chuck's white cane slides from side to side. It taps the shelf on this side then the shelf on that side. The tap tells him if there is a thing in his path.

The tap of the cane is like the ping of a sub or the squeak of a bat. It tells Chuck if he must walk a small bit or a lot.

Jeff walks in back of Chuck. He keeps his hand on Chuck's back. This way he does not need his cane. He trusts Chuck will keep him safe. Chuck hits a box on the rug and he and Jeff walk past it.

Jazmin takes the filmstrip to a desk. There is a black and gray thing on the desk and a small screen.

"This is where you put the filmstrip. We will get to see it on this screen," Jazmin says. She helps Jeff and Chuck put their hands on the filmstrip screen so they can feel it.

"Will people talk while you see it?" Jeff asks.

"No. I do not have the tape. I hope there will be text on the filmstrip," Jazmin says.

Jazmin puts the filmstrip into the gray and black thing. It gets stuck. "This has a problem. I cannot get it. It could take some time." She slides the filmstrip in here and in there.

The kids wait. Then they wait. Still they must wait. Jazmin cannot get the filmstrip in. She goes to get Jill.

The Wait

The kids walk from here to there in the basement. Chuck and Jeff's canes go tap, tap, tap, tap.

There is so much dust. The smell is bad. They walk to a desk. "I see a box of snapshots," Lil says She and Liz pick up one snapshot then the next.

"This is odd," Liz says.

"What is odd?" Chuck asks.

"This snapshot. That could be Mr. Ling's grandchild," Liz says as she holds the snapshot.

"May I see?" Lil asks. Liz hands her the snapshot.

Lil scans the snapshot. "That could be Edwin Ling, but this is an old snapshot. Edwin Ling is in his teens like this kid. This snapshot is way old for it to be Edwin."

"Jill got it to go," Jazmin calls to the kids.

Liz, Jeff, and Chuck go to Jazmin.

Lil stands still and scans the snapshot that she holds. It could be Edwin Ling. He has on a black top and jeans. A long rope is slung 'cross his chest.

There is a lamp set next to the teen. He has lots of mud on him. It is as if he had lain in the mud. He has on a helmet with a cave lamp.

Lil stands still and scans the snapshot that she holds.

The kid has a big smile. He holds a thing in his hand, but Lil cannot tell what it is. She cannot tell what is on his feet. They have lots of mud on them.

Lil twists to go to Jazmin and the rest of the kids. She trips and falls. She is flat on the rug. The smell is bad.

Jazmin and Liz run to her.

"Are you OK?" Jazmin asks.

"Yes, but can you smell that? It is BAD!" Lil says.

Jazmin and Liz bend down. "Yuck," they each say.

"That is the dankest mold smell," Jazmin says. "Where does it come from?"

They all see if they can find the smell. Jeff and Chuck's canes tap as they walk from here to there.

"The smell is the strongest here," Jeff says.

The rest of them come up to Jeff.

"There is an exit. It seems to be shut. The desk and shelf block it, but I see it in back of this shelf," Liz says.

"Yes, I would think that is an exit that is shut," Jazmin says.

"The exit at the back of the basement says, 'EXIT' at the top. It is lit in red. This exit does not have EXIT on top of it. It is not lit up. I did not think they could block an exit with a shelf," Liz says.

"They should not block exits," Jazmin says. "Exits should be free to get to. If we need to get out fast, the shelf would be in our way."

Lil and Liz gaze at the shelf that blocks the exit. Jeff sets his hands on the shelf to feel it. He shrugs when he cannot find an exit.

"Mom, did you see this?" Liz says.

Lil hands the snapshot to Jazmin. "We think it is Mr. Ling's grandkid, Edwin, but that does not seem like it could be."

Jazmin gazes at the snapshot. "That is not Edwin. That must be Mr. Ling when he was a teen. Where did you find it? I bet Mr. Ling would like to see it."

"It was in that box," Lil says. "Can we ask my mom if we can take it to him?"

Jazmin nods. "Yes, you can ask her. Come see the filmstrip. There are snapshots of oxen back when **The Dog Wog Pet Shop** was **The Quail Spring Ranch.**"

"Mom, I do not want to see the filmstrip. I do not like this basement. I feel odd in here. That smell is bad and I do not like that there is a shelf that blocks the exit," Liz says.

"I do not like it in here as well," Chuck says.

"OK. We can go. I got the name of the leaf I will plant to keep Anvil and Magnet well," Jazmin says.

Tandem Bikes

Lil and Liz ask if they can ride their bikes to see Mr. Ling. "Wait. Then Jeff and Chuck could not go with us," Lil says.

"Chuck and I have bikes. They are tandem bikes," Jeff says.

"You can each ride with one of us. Jeff and I will sit in the back. You can each hold the handgrips and take us where we need to go," Chuck says.

The kids walk to Chuck and Jeff's to get the bikes that each have two seats and three wheels. Jazmin will stay at Jill's home until they get back. She has stuff she must read on her laptop for her job.

The kids put on their bike helmets and ride uphill to Mr. Ling's fish shed.

"I had so much fun at his wing ding shin dig in May," Lil says. "He would beat on the drum and I would hop and skip. My dress would twist this way and that way. I hope you can come when he has his next wing ding shin dig."

"That would be grand," Liz says as she and Chuck make his bike go up the big hill.

"We went to his wing ding shin dig last fall," Jeff says. "It was lots of fun. I could not go to the one in May. I had to get lots of sleep. My chess team had a big game the next day."

At the fish shed, they take off their helmets and hang them from their bikes. Liz goes to click down the kickstand to make Chuck's bike stand still. Then she thinks that she does not have to do that. Chuck's bike has three wheels. It will not fall on its side.

Chuck's bike has three wheels. It will not fall on its side.

Jeff's cane goes tap, tap, tap, tap as he walks to the fish shed. This time he leads and Chuck walks in back of him. Chuck trusts Jeff will not let him trip.

Lil rings the fish shed bell.

Mr. Ling comes to let them in. "Lil, Liz, Chuck, and Jeff. I am so glad to see you. Come in, come in. Did you come to feed some cress to the fish and frogs?"

"May we?" Liz asks. "I like to feed pets, but I do not get to do it much."

Mr. Ling smiles. "Liz, you have Ms. Jolt the dog, Chad the cat, a set of oxen, a colt, chickens and I cannot list what pets I have not met. You think you do not get to feed pets much?"

Liz shrugs. "Well, it does not seem like much to me."

Mr. Ling leads the kids to the back of his fish shed. It smells dank like the basement of **The Public Hall for Tomes of Tales**. There is lots of water here so it does not seem odd to have that smell.

Mr. Ling lets the kids pick fresh cress and toss it into the pond. The frogs say, "Trib, trib, ribbit, ribbit." The fish leap and splash.

"Mr. Ling, I like it here so much," Liz says.

Mr. Ling smiles.

"The basement at **The Public Hall for Tomes of Tales** smells like this, but I do not like it there. It feels odd there," Liz says.

Mr. Ling's smile stops. "You should not go in that basement. That smell there is not the same as this smell. You cannot say they are the same." He grabs a bit of cress and drops some in the pond.

Liz gazes at Lil. Lil puts her hands in her pockets. They cannot think what makes Mr. Ling seem so odd.

"We went to the basement with Aunt Jazmin," Jeff says.

Mr. Ling's hand holds still. "What did you do in the basement?"

"Mom had to find a plant to keep my oxen well," Liz says.

Mr. Ling nods and feeds his fish. He seems upset.

The Snapshot

Lil gets the snapshot from her backpack. "This was in a box in the basement. My mom said we could bring it here for you to see. We have to take it back to her, but I hope you are glad to see it."

Mr. Ling does not drop cress into the pond. He holds still. His gaze is on the snapshot. He drops the cress in the pond and wipes his hand on his pant leg. His gaze is still on the snapshot.

Lil hands the snapshot to him. Mr. Ling takes the snapshot. His cheeks go white. He sits on a bench next to the pond.

Lil sits next to him. "Are you OK? Is this you? What did you do to get so much mud on you?"

"It is late. That is a long tale. You must go home while there is still sun. I will tell you about this the next time I see you." Mr. Ling stands up.

Lil sits next to him. "Are you OK? Is this you? What did you do to get so much mud on you?"

"Come, you must go. Thank you. I will take this snapshot back to **The Public Hall for Tomes of Tales**. I must go there to check out a thing or two. I can take it back then. Thank you for your trip here. You must go home," Mr. Ling says. He takes the kids to their bikes. Then he goes back into the fish shed.

There is a click, click. The kids can tell that was a twist of the lock.

"That is odd. Mr. Ling does not lock his fish shed. He wants it to be safe for the fish. If he does not lock it, people could help his fish if there was a problem," Lil says.

"This is not OK. What if they find out?" Mr. Ling says from inside the fish shed. His tone is soft, but the kids can tell that is what he said.

Lil is sad. Liz cannot think what to do. Chuck and Jeff cannot think what to say.

"Let us ride to your home. We can come back the next day we are with you. That is an old snapshot. Mr. Ling must have felt a shock to see himself with so much mud and a rope," Liz says.

Chuck nods. Jeff says, "We can do that." Lil gazes at the fish shed.

The kids put on their helmets and get on their bikes. They ride to Lil's home. They cannot think what upset Mr. Ling and made him be so odd. They think it could be bad or sad. Each of them thinks of what they must do.

This is not the end.
You can read
The Hidden Tale 2
in Step 10.

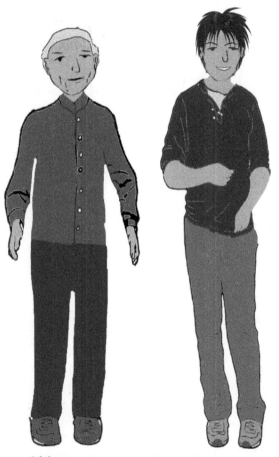

Old Mr. Ling   Mr. Ling when he was a teen

Sight Words Used In:
"The Snapshot"

a, about, are, as, aunt, be, come, comes, could, cousin, cousins, do, does, down, for, friend, friend's, from, go, goes, has, have, he, her, here, hi, his, I, into, is, island, me, Mr., Ms., my, no, of, OK, one, or, our, out, people, please, put, puts, said, says, she, should, so, some, talk, the, their, there, they, to, TV, two, walk, walks, was, water, we, where, would, you, your

Approximately 3,370 words

Keywords

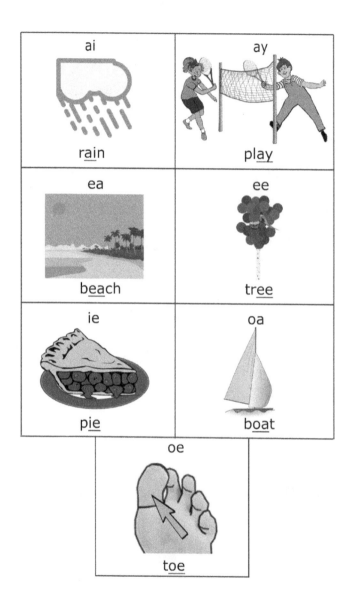

ai	ay
r<u>ai</u>n	pl<u>ay</u>

ea	ee
b<u>ea</u>ch	tr<u>ee</u>

ie	oa
p<u>ie</u>	b<u>oa</u>t

oe
t<u>oe</u>

DOG ON A LOG Books
Phonics Progression

DOG ON A LOG Pup Books
Book 1
Phonological/Phonemic Awareness:
- Words
- Rhyming
- Syllables, identification, blending, segmenting
- Identifying individual letter sounds

Books 2-3
Phonemic Awareness/Phonics
- Consonants, primary sounds
- Short vowels
- Blending
- Introduction to sight words

DOG ON A LOG Let's GO! and Chapter Books

Step 1
- Consonants, primary sounds
- Short vowels
- Digraphs: ch, sh, th, wh, ck
- 2 and 3 sound words
- Possessive 's

Step 2
- Bonus letters (f, l, s, z after short vowel)
- "all"
- –s suffix

Step 3
- Letter Buddies: ang, ing, ong, ung, ank, ink, onk, unk

Step 4
- Consonant blends to make 4 sound words
- 3 and 4 sound words ending in –lk, -sk

Step 5
- Digraph blend –nch to make 3 and 4 sound words
- Silent e, including "-ke"

Step 6
- Exception words containing: ild, old, olt, ind, ost

Step 7
- 5 sounds in a closed syllable word plus suffix -s (crunch, slumps)
- 3 letter blends and up to 6 sounds in a closed syllable word (script, spring)

Step 8

- Two-syllable words with 2 closed syllables, not blends (sunset, chicken, unlock)

Step 9

- Two-syllable words with all previously introduced sounds including blends, exception words, and silent "e" (blacksmith, kindness, inside)
- Vowel digraphs: ai, ay, ea, ee, ie, oa, oe (rain, play, beach, tree, pie, boat, toe)

WATCH FOR MORE STEPS COMING SOON

**Let's GO! Books
have less text**

**Chapter Books
are longer**

DOG ON A LOG Books
Sight Word Progression

DOG ON A LOG Pup Books
a, does, go, has, her is, of, says, the, to

DOG ON A LOG Let's GO! and
Chapter Books

Step 1
a, and, are, be, does, go, goes, has, he, her, his, into, is, like, my, of, OK, says, see, she, the, they, to, want, you

Step 2
could, do, eggs, for, from, have, here, I, likes, me, nest, onto, or, puts, said, say, sees, should, wants, was, we, what, would, your

Step 3
as, Mr., Mrs., no, put, their, there, where

Step 4
push, saw

Step 5
come, comes, egg, pull, pulls, talk, walk, walks

Step 6
Ms., so, some, talks

Step 7
Hmmm, our, out, Pop E., TV

Step 8
Dr., friend, full, hi, island, people, please

Step 9
about, aunt, cousin, cousins, down, friends, hi, inn, know, knows, me, one, ones, TVs, two, water, welcome

More DOG ON A LOG Books

Most books available in Paperback, Hardback, and e-book formats

DOG ON A LOG Parent and Teacher Guides

Book 1 (Also in FREE e-book and PDF Bookfold)
- Teaching a Struggling Reader: One Mom's Experience with Dyslexia

Book 2 (FREE e-book and PDF Bookfold only)
- How to Use Decodable Books to Teach Reading

DOG ON A LOG Pup Books
Book 1
- Before the Squiggle Code (A Roadmap to Reading)

Books 2-3
- The Squiggle Code (Letters Make Words)
- Kids' Squiggles (Letters Make Words)

DOG ON A LOG Let's GO! and Chapter Books

Step 1
- The Dog on the Log
- The Pig Hat
- Chad the Cat
- Zip the Bug
- The Fish and the Pig

Step 2
- Mud on the Path
- The Red Hen
- The Hat and Bug Shop
- Babs the 'Bot
- The Cub

Step 3
- Mr. Bing has Hen Dots
- The Junk Lot Cat
- Bonk Punk Hot Rod
- The Ship with Wings
- The Sub in the Fish Tank

Step 4
- The Push Truck
- The Sand Hill
- Lil Tilt and Mr. Ling
- Musk Ox in the Tub
- The Trip to the Pond

Step 5
- Bake a Cake
- The Crane at the Cave
- Ride a Bike
- Crane or Crane?
- The Swing Gate

Step 6

- The Colt
- The Gold Bolt
- Hide in the Blinds
- The Stone Child
- Tolt the Kind Cat

Step 7

- Quest for A Grump Grunt
- The Blimp
- The Spring in the Lane
- Stamp for a Note
- Stripes and Splats

Step 8

- Anvil and Magnet
- The Mascot
- Kevin's Rabbit Hole
- The Humbug Vet and Medic Shop
- Chickens in the Attic

Step 9

- Trip to Cactus Gulch 1: The Step-Up Team
- Trip to Cactus Gulch 2: Into the Mineshaft
- Play the Bagpipes
- The Hidden Tale 1: The Lost Snapshot

All chapter books can be purchased individually or with all the same-step books in one volume.

Steps 1-5 can be bought as Let's GO! Books which are less text companions to the chapter books.

All titles can be bought as chapter books.

WATCH FOR MORE BOOKS COMING SOON

How You Can Help

Parents often worry that their child (or even adult learner) is not going to learn to read. Hearing other people's successes (especially when they struggled) can give worried parents or teachers hope. I would encourage others to share their experiences with products you've used by posting reviews at your favorite bookseller(s) stating how your child benefitted from those books or materials (whether it was DOG ON A LOG Books or another book or product.) This will help other parents and teachers know which products they should consider using. More than that, hearing your successes could truly help another family feel hopeful. It's amazing that something as seemingly small as a review can ease someone's concerns.

Photograph Credits

Thank you to the following photographers for allowing me to use their awesome photographs. Most required modifications so they would synch with the stories and desert locations. I am truly appreciative of the photographers allowing me to do so.

(Standing) Mule photograph
modified from original by
Danilo Tic
via www.flickr.com
Made available by
https://creativecommons.org/licenses/by-sa/2.0/

(Head down) The Mule and the Crow photograph
Modified from original by
Loco Steve
via www.flickr.com
Made available by
https://creativecommons.org/licenses/by/2.0/

Serenading the Sunset
(cover and inside bagpiper photo)
modified from original
via www.flickr.com
Made available by direct permission of
Photographer Jo Ann Deasy

Sunset Serenade
(Play the Bagpipes cover image)
modified from original
via www.flickr.com
Made available by direct permission of
Photographer Steve Jurveston

Public Domain "Spring" photo from
www.pixabay.com

TROON BOYS BRIGADE PIPE BAND
photograph
Modified from original by
Freddie Phillips
via www.flickr.com
Made available by
https://creativecommons.org/licenses/by/
2.0/

DOG ON A LOG
Quick Assessment

Have your child read the following words. If they can't read every word in a Step, that is probably where in the series they should start. Some children may benefit starting at an earlier step to help them build confidence in their reading abilities.

Get a printable assessment sheet at:
www.dogonalogbooks.com/how-to-use/assessment-tool/

Step 1
fin, mash, sock, sub, cat, that, Dan's

Step 2
less, bats, tell, mall, chips, whiff, falls

Step 3
bangs, dank, honk, pings, chunk, sink, gong, rungs

Step 4
silk, fluff, smash, krill, drop, slim, whisk

Step 5
hunch, crate, rake, tote, inch, mote, lime

Step 6
child, molts, fold, hind, jolt, post, colds

Step 7

strive, scrape, splint, twists, crunch, prints, blend

Step 8

finish, denim, within, bathtub, sunset, medic, habit

Step 9

hundred, goldfinch, free, wheat, inhale, play, Joe

Step 10

be, remake, spry, repeat, silo, sometime, pinwheel

WATCH FOR MORE STEPS COMING SOON

CPSIA information can be obtained
at www.ICGtesting.com
Printed in the USA
LVHW111748010223
738416LV00002B/124